GW01161861

Original title:
The Stillness of Winter Days

Copyright © 2024 Creative Arts Management OÜ
All rights reserved.

Author: Juliette Kensington
ISBN HARDBACK: 978-9916-94-582-7
ISBN PAPERBACK: 978-9916-94-583-4

Resting in the Quiet

Snowflakes fall with a plop,
Sleds go zooming, then stop.
A squirrel in a fuzzy hat,
Parking his rear on a mat.

Icicles hang like sharp teeth,
The winds whisper a frosty wreath.
My cheeks are rosy like a cherry,
But my nose feels rather merry!

Hot cocoa spills, oh what a sight,
Marshmallows dance, a fluffy flight.
While mittens battle, oh what fun,
Lost one again? Come on, just one!

We leap in piles of snowy fluff,
Building snowmen, oh that's tough.
They stand tall, then fall like bricks,
Winter's playground, full of tricks!

Shadows Upon the Hearth

In the corner sits a cat,
Purring loud, it's quite the brat.
Chasing shadows on the wall,
Taking tumbles, what a fall!

Socks on feet, a daring dance,
Slipping 'round, a wild prance.
The fire crackles, laughs ignite,
Who knew winter could be light?

Threads of White

Snowflakes twirl like silly hats,
Dancing down with giggles, splats.
Building snowmen, not so grand,
One looks like a giant hand!

Hot cocoa splashes, marshmallows fly,
Giggles echo, oh my, oh my!
Outside, snowballs fly with glee,
A war declared! Just wait and see!

Enchanted by Stillness

Inside the house, we cozy up,
Wrapped in blankets, sip from cups.
The dog snores loud, what a tune,
Dreaming of chasing bunnies soon!

On the fridge, a snowman's face,
Constructed by a toddler's grace.
With a carrot nose and lopsided grin,
He'll melt come spring, oh where to begin?

Celestial White

Stars are frozen in the night,
Twinkling down, oh what a sight!
The owl hoots, a comical scroll,
Wonders where he lost his soul!

Footprints lead to nowhere's end,
Chased by snow, a playful trend.
Clouds above bring flurries, cheer,
Catch a laugh, winter's near!

The Quiet of Bare Branches

In crisp air, the trees not dressed,
They wiggle their fingers, feeling stressed.
Squirrels wonder where nuts went,
While birds audition for best lament.

A statue of a cat, frozen in glee,
Chasing visions of mice, can't you see?
Hiccuping snowflakes dance from the sky,
While old man winter just laughs by.

Frost Kisses on Sleeping Ground

The earth wears a blanket, quite absurd,
Yet it snores beneath, not making a word.
A bunny hops, slips, and goes 'whoa!'
While ice skates giggle in the glow.

Teeth chattering like an old tin can,
I'm dressed like a marshmallow, oh man!
Penguins slide by, their tuxedos neat,
I trip on a puddle, a real ice treat!

Breath of the Season's Serenity

In puffy coats, we waddle like ducks,
Guitar-playing snowmen chuckle with pluck.
Pine trees whisper secrets into the breeze,
While icicles dangle, taking their ease.

The sun sneaks out for a quick little peek,
But we shiver in shadows, feeling quite meek.
A hot cocoa hug warms frosty toes,
As marshmallows float in a comical pose.

Hours Wrapped in Icy Silence

Time ticks slowly in denim-thick air,
While errands await with a frozen stare.
A snowman frowns, feeling a bit blue,
As kids zip past, not saying 'boo.'

The clock strikes five, but the sun won't budge,
Yet still, here we sip, refusing to judge.
In this frozen fun, we laugh 'til we cry,
For even cold days can be warm, oh my!

When Nature Takes a Breath

Trees are napping, all leaves tucked in,
Snowflakes dance, like they've had too much gin.
Squirrels wear scarves, looking quite bold,
Racing down branches, like stories retold.

Marshmallow clouds drift, oh so slow,
They tickle each other, putting on a show.
Frosty characters in this chilly play,
With every breath, they giggle and sway.

Echoing Embers

Fireside chat with the crackle and pop,
Even the shadows are wanting to hop.
Coco cups stumble, spill sweet delight,
While marshmallows plot a sugary bite.

The cat plays it cool, stretched all the way,
While dogs dream of chasing snowballs all day.
Life's a cozy riddle, each laugh a spark,
In the warmth of the home, it's never too dark.

The Beauty of Waiting

Snowflakes mimic stars, just not so bright,
Anticipation lingers, a teasing delight.
Icicles hang, forming a crystal display,
While we count the days in a frosty ballet.

Birds in the trees wear their best winter coats,
Chirping like choirs on magical floats.
We twiddle our thumbs, with glee in our hearts,
As winter plays tricks, and excitement imparts.

Glacial Stillness

Ponds wearing blankets much thicker than fluff,
Penguins slide in, shouting, 'This ain't so tough!'
But snowmen hold secrets, never to share,
With carrot noses, they look so debonair.

Chill in the air makes cheeks rosy and round,
Kids throw snowballs that make silly sounds.
In this frozen kingdom, laughter takes flight,
While snowflakes whisper, 'Isn't this just right?"

Through the Fog of December Dreams

Cats in sweaters prance with glee,
Jingle bells stuck in a tree.
Snowmen wobble, hats askew,
As frosty air whispers, "What's new?"

Mittens lost, toast burnt and dry,
Sipping cocoa, we let out a sigh.
Laughter echoes through the haze,
In this fog of winter's playful maze.

Still Waters Under a Frosted Sky

Ice skating squirrels try to glide,
Amidst the snowflakes, they take pride.
Mice on skates, such a sight to see,
Zooming past with glee and esprit.

Under the frost, a puddle's grin,
Splashing about, it draws us in.
Unexpected joy in each slide and fall,
Winter's grip can't freeze our all.

A Canvas of Stillness and Light

Brush of white on roofs so high,
Even the cats won't dare to try.
Frosted trees stand tall in line,
While the birds huddle, drinking wine.

Chickens march, all feathers and fuss,
Looking puzzled by the icy bus.
Toasty hats upon our heads,
In this world where whimsy spreads.

A Breath of Winter's Breath

Nose red like Rudolf's, oh so bright,
As we dash around, giving a fright.
Snowball fights, laughter on the way,
Winter's breath's just here to play.

Under blankets piled so high,
We watch snowflakes drift and fly.
A dance, a shuffle, winter's jest,
These frosty days are the very best!

A Blanket of Quiet

Snowflakes fluff their fluffy tails,
As squirrels slide on icy trails.
Frosty breaths become a dance,
While penguins practice their romance.

Hot cocoa sips, a warming cheer,
As snowmen grin from ear to ear.
Chubby cheeks turn bright and red,
With fright at what the median said!

Echoes of Icy Pines

A rabbit hops, slips, and trips,
While penguins gather for their quips.
Trees wear coats of spun-out snow,
Whisper jokes as breezes blow.

Icicles hang like nature's fangs,
While birds make silly, frozen clangs.
The pine trees tickle with their cones,
As squirrels claim them as their homes.

Tranquil Shadows

Laughter echoes through the chill,
In snowball fights, we get our fill.
Penguins march like tiny troops,
While hot chocolate makes us droop.

The frost makes everything a pop,
As winter vibes just never stop.
With snowflakes laughing on our nose,
We dance like clumsy, jolly pros!

Hushed Heartbeats of December

The world is dressed in white and sweet,
As snowmen compete for the best feat.
With carrot noses, they strike a pose,
While winter laughs in chilly prose.

Sipping cocoa, we share our tales,
And plot the best of snowball trails.
A slip, a fall, a joyful shout,
In this realm, there's never doubt!

Frost-kissed Reveries

Cold toes peeking from my bed,
I dream of snowflakes on my head.
A squirrel slides down a frozen tree,
I laugh, oh what a sight to see.

Hot cocoa spills right on my pants,
The dog prances in a snowball dance.
Frosty air fills up my nose,
Coughing loudly as the laughter grows.

Snowmen wear my old scarf tight,
I think they might just win a fight!
With carrot noses, they decree,
They're far too cool to even see!

Icicles hang like teeth of fate,
They drip on cars, oh what a fate!
In winter's grip, we smile and cheer,
For fun and folly, winter's here!

Crystal Dreams Unfold

Morning light gleams on the street,
I slip and slide like I'm on feet.
The world is blank, a canvas white,
Snowball fights? Oh what a delight!

My mittens, lost, are now a myth,
Hiding under snow, like some kind of gift.
I take a pic of frozen air,
Who knew this chill could bring such flare?

Snowflakes twirl like little stars,
While I make plans for snow-formed cars.
But they melt down to watery pools,
I guess it's time for snowman rules!

With every laugh and snowy cheer,
I'll toast to winter, never fear.
In crystal dreams, let's make some noise,
For warmth is found in playful joys!

Solitude in the Snowfall

In a world so quiet, tricks unwind,
Snowflakes whisper secrets, so kind.
A cat leaps high in frosty glee,
    I giggle as it lands on me!

Crunchy boots on hidden trails,
The wind tells tales, it never fails.
With every step, the world feels wide,
    Too bad my nose cannot abide!

My neighbor's cat, all bundled up,
    Looks like a fluffball in a cup.
She gives a snooty little glare,
As if she knows I'm unaware!

In snowfall's grip, we find delight,
Breath like clouds in morning light.
Through icy streets, we roam and play,
    Winter's antics brighten our day!

A Time to Reflect

As I sip tea, the cup goes cold,
My thoughts drift back to tales retold.
Snowmen sit with grins so wide,
Somehow I feel they're on my side!

Under the porch, a rabbit hops,
With ears so big, he nearly flops.
I chuckle softly, he looks like me,
In this grand winter jubilee!

The fridge is stocked with sweets galore,
But snowflakes stop me at the door.
I chomp on chocolate, a festive snack,
Then grin when I hear the door go whack!

So here I sit, a cheerful mess,
In winter's grip, I feel so blessed.
Let laughter ring, a shining bell,
For in the snow, we laugh so well!

Quietude of the Hearth

In the corner, the cat's taking a nap,
While the dog blames the snow for the lack of a trap.
Grandma's knitting a hat, oh what a sight,
It's lopsided like me on a not-so-great night.

Coffee's boiling over, a dance gone wrong,
I laugh at the squirrels, so cheerful and strong.
Pajamas are rumpled, all warm and cuddly,
Here's to the fire, the glow's quite cuddly.

Lonesome Nights

The fridge hums a tune, a lone serenade,
I giggle at shadows that dance in the shade.
The moon's peeking in, my late-night friend,
Playing tag with the clouds, no need to pretend.

My socks are mismatched, but who even cares?
I shiver and laugh at my unkempt hair.
Hot cocoa spills like my hopes for great cheer,
At least the marshmallows are still quite near.

Embracing the Void

In the endless quiet, the clock ticks slow,
I'd swear it's the ice that's stealing the show.
Out in the yard, a snowman's taking a fall,
He never stood a chance; he was barely tall.

I try to persuade my blanket to stay,
But it just keeps slipping, running away.
I might start a dance with my pajama pants,
But it's too cold for spontaneity's prance.

Winter's Gentle Caress

A snowflake lands right on my nose,
What a gentle tickle, it giggles and goes.
Outside, the kids tumble, a laughter-filled spree,
While I'm here contemplating what else I could be.

I slip on the sidewalk, quite the graceful thud,
The snowman now laughs; he's covered in mud.
With a sigh and a chuckle, I'd rather not freeze,
But winter's just one long, hilarious tease.

The Language of Snow

Once snowflakes dropped with a plop,
They giggled as they made a stop.
They whispered secrets in a flurry,
Beneath the trees, they danced in a hurry.

Snowmen wear hats and frown-shaped smiles,
They wobble and wobble for quite a while.
With carrot noses, they tell snow jokes,
While snowball fights amuse all the folks.

Penguins slide down the icy hills,
With slippery moves, they bring us thrills.
They chuckle and tumble in the crisp air,
While children giggle, their laughter rare.

As icicles form like frozen teeth,
They dangle and sway beneath our feet.
In the valley, the snowflakes play peek,
In frosty showers of laughter they sneak.

The Calm Before Thaw

Under the sun, the ice starts to crack,
As winter prepares to give summer a whack.
The squirrels are plotting their next grand heist,
While the birds are dreaming of juicy rice.

We wait for warmth with bated breath,
As frost giants prepare to meet their death.
The snowmen cry, their arms in despair,
For soon they'll melt into thin air.

The laughter from children jumps in delight,
As they make angels before taking flight.
In this moment of truce, all seems so bright,
But don't let the sunshine steal the night.

The weather may tease with a wink and a grin,
As spring creeps in, letting the fun begin.
But for now, we dance on this icy ballet,
And bask in the joys of our winter's sway.

Emptiness Embraced

In the barren trees, where laughter is rare,
The wind tells jokes with a chilly flair.
Footprints are sketching stories untold,
Of snowball mischief that never gets old.

Inside our homes, we gather near,
With hot cocoa cheers, the warmth we endear.
We laugh at the snowflakes, each one unique,
As they dress up our world with their frosty sneak peak.

The quiet hush hides giggles of glee,
As winter's cloak wraps each branch of the tree.
Emptiness hums like a quirky old tune,
While cats chase the shadows beneath the full moon.

Snow days bring treasures of childhood delight,
With warmth in our hearts through the frostbitten night.
We embrace the chill with a shrug and a smile,
For emptiness means we can play for a while!

Whispering Winds of January

January winds come waltzing through,
With whispers of mischief and secrets anew.
They tickle the nose of the unsuspecting,
And send all the haters to go defecting.

Snowflakes swirl as they dance in the air,
Plotting their landings with delicate care.
They giggle as they land on a squirrel's head,
While chattering critters tell tales for the dead.

When the world turns white and the skies go grey,
The laughter of winter will sweep you away.
With mittens on hands and boots on our feet,
We stomp through the snow to a jolly old beat.

Oh, how the winds tease with each chilly gust,
As icicles shimmer with frosty lust.
So let us don scarves and join in the play,
For January's magic is fleeting, they say.

Whispers of Frosted Mornings

A snowman stands, with a crooked grin,
His carrot nose looks like it's about to spin.
With mittens on, I take a slip,
And land right down, my coffee in a drip.

The trees are dressed, oh what a sight,
Their branches stiff, trying hard to fight.
Birds are chirping, their beaks all frosty,
I swear they're laughing, oh so costly!

A frostbitten squirrel scurries by,
With cheeks so stuffed, I can't help but sigh.
He pauses for a moment, looks my way,
Did he just wink? Or am I just sway?

I wave at snowflakes, as they caper down,
Wearing my boots, I look like a clown.
In this chilly wonderland, life's a play,
Each frozen giggle brightens the gray.

Silent Pines Beneath a Blanket of Snow

Pines look regal, they stand in a row,
While I, in warm clothes, seem to steal the show.
Snowflakes tumble, like feathers from a bird,
My hat flies off! Did I just hear a word?

A burly man struggles with his sled,
It flips and flops, landing him in red.
His dog just smiles, tongue out in fun,
Chasing after snowballs, on the run!

The air is crisp, a joke that's well shared,
As snowmen plot how to catch me unprepared.
They whisper secrets, while I sip my tea,
With marshmallows floating, just like me!

I toss a snowball, but miss the mark,
It hits a tree, and leaves a snowy spark.
Laughter echoes, as my friends cheer on,
In this frozen paradise, identity's gone.

Echoes in the Crystal Air

The sun peeks out, through clouds so fluffy,
Winter's breath makes everything fluffy.
Hot cocoa stirs, with a lot of flair,
Who knew a mug could have such a dare?

Two friends in boots waddle like penguins,
Each step they take, they knock off their dens.
Snowflakes land, tickling noses to giggle,
One sneezes loud, sending snow snow-diggle.

A plaid scarf flies, rebel in the breeze,
Chasing the wind, like it's something to seize.
The snow globe spins, a tempest of delight,
"Catch me if you can!" yells in the twilight.

In this frosty playground, jokes unfold,
Every slip a laugh, every fall a gold.
Beneath this canopy, winter does play,
With echoes of joy in the cold ballet.

Veils of Ice and Solitude

Icicles hang like chandeliers of fun,
While a snow-covered bench sits under the sun.
I plop myself down, a cushy delight,
And slide right off — what a comedic sight!

A cat prances by, with swagger unmatched,
He slips on the ice, and chaos is hatched.
With a scrunch of the nose, he stands up tall,
Then glances at me, as if to call!

Snowballs fly like cannonballs of cheer,
Twirling around like we have no fear.
We're children again, in the frigid glow,
Making snow angels while avoiding a show.

With peace in the air, yet laughter so free,
Moments crafted like art, fluid and carefree.
In this realm of frost, where mirth takes its flight,
Joy dances, even in the still, chilly light.

Dreams Wrapped in White

Snowflakes dance in crazy loops,
Frosty noses and chilly scoops.
A snowman wears a carrot hat,
But tripped on ice—oh, how he sat!

Sledding down the hill like mad,
Wheels fall off and isn't that sad?
Hot cocoa spills on the fluffy ground,
Laughter echoes, a joyful sound.

Winter's chill wraps us in cheer,
Penguins slip, but don't show fear.
An avalanche of snowballs flies,
I'm the target—oh, what a surprise!

But here we are, cheers all around,
Chasing the dog who's lost and found.
With jokes that no one else can hear,
Winter brings us all good cheer!

Solace in the Chill

Icicles hang like a frozen twist,
Snowflakes whisper, can't be missed.
Penguin impersonators all around,
Strut on ice while doing a bound!

Coffee breath turns into clouds,
As people shout and form loud crowds.
Cheese hats perched on frozen heads,
Makes one wonder, 'What's in their breads?'

Snowball fights with zero aim,
Hit the cat; oh, what a shame!
With laughter ringing through the trees,
It's hard to feel the biting breeze.

Winter days are just a game,
With tickles, snowballs, and a fame.
As the sun dips, watch shadows play,
What a funny, frosty day!

Serene Evenings

The night falls soft like a pillow,
And snowflakes land on the wise old willow.
A squirrel skis down a twinkling slope,
Wearing shades and a scarf—oh, the hope!

Hot soup awaits in my cozy chair,
But watch out for splashes everywhere!
The cat leaps high to catch a flake,
And ends up wrapped in a snowy wake.

Lights twinkle like stars, what a sight,
The raccoon decides it's time for a bite.
What's that sound? A clatter near,
The neighbor slipped—oh dear oh dear!

Under the moon, our laughter thrums,
While snowmen dance, looking quite dumb.
With spirits high and hearts aglow,
These winter evenings steal the show!

A Nurturing Cold

Under blankets snugly tucked,
Winter wraps us, feeling plucked.
Frosty faces in balmy socks,
Inventing games with paper blocks.

Snowshoes dance on powder white,
Oh wait, that's just my dog in flight!
Noses red, cheeks like cherries,
We build a fort, then launch our queries.

Winter fairies with clumsy wings,
Create magic with tiny flings.
But wait! A tumble and a fall,
The funniest thing in the mall!

As we share grins and funny tales,
The cold's embrace never fails.
With warmth and folly, we're not alone,
In this frosty castle, we've found our throne!

Cold Breath of Dawn

Frosty air gives a chilly laugh,
My nose is red, what a silly gaffe!
Birds in the trees look like ice cubes,
Checkbox in hand, they've sealed their grubes.

Pants snug, I hop like a bumbling frog,
Amongst flurries, dancing a snow-booted clog.
Winter's dance floor is fully booked,
No refunds given, you're all just hooked!

A mug of cocoa spills on my fluff,
With marshmallows that look quite tough.
They float like tiny, white snowdrifts,
In a world where laughter is winter's gifts.

Faded Footprints

Giggles trail where I stumbled and slipped,
Like a snowman that wildly flipped.
Footprints fade, oh where did they go?
Lost in the giggles of winter's show.

Sledding down hills with a goofy shout,
Came up with a face full of snow, no doubt!
My cheeks are pink, a rosy delight,
Who needs a gym? This is pure winter fight!

In a snowball war, I took a stand,
Only to trip, face-first in the sand.
Well, they say winter's a time to be bold,
But my belly flopped made stories unfold.

A World Frozen in Time

Icicles hung like a frozen giggle,
They glint in the sun, a good old wiggle.
Snowflakes whisper with flurries of cheer,
Creating a world where laughter is near.

Penguins waddle like they've lost the plot,
Awkward and funny, it's quite a lot!
Snowmen stand guard with carrot noses,
Gazing at snowball fights, striking poses!

Time stands still as socks are knee-high,
With mismatched patterns that catch the eye.
But who cares, we're warm in our silly get-up,
Drinking hot cocoa from an oversized cup!

The Warmth of Distant Firelight

Fires crackle with a playful shout,
While the cats act like they're all about.
Huddled in blankets, a cuddly brigade,
Sipping on cocoa, plans we've made!

The marshmallows roast with a happy cheer,
Watch out! One might just disappear!
With giggles and chatters ringing the night,
It's warm as laughter, the best kind of light.

Chasing shadows that flicker and dance,
With footed pajamas, we twirl and prance.
Oh winter, you jester, with your snowy jest,
Bringing us merriment, a cozy quest!

Shimmering Silence

Cold air whispers, yet we chat,
A snowman dances, fancy that!
Wooly hats reluctantly worn,
Snowflakes giggle, winter's scorn.

Boots slip-slide on icy ground,
Laughter echoes all around.
Hot cocoa spills, marshmallows fly,
Winter's waltz makes time pass by.

Frosty breath, a dragon's flare,
Sledding down without a care.
Trees wear coats of fluffy white,
We chuckle, 'Isn't this delight?'

Winter's pranks, it's all in fun,
Chasing snowballs, never done.
In this quiet, frosty game,
Who knew winter could be so tame?

Veil of Frost

Blankets of white, the world so bright,
Snowflakes tumble, pure delight.
A cat slides past, a comic scene,
Chasing shadows, oh so keen.

Windy whispers, secrets told,
A snowball fight, courageous bold.
Eyes like saucers, laughter loud,
Winter mischief, oh so proud.

Hot soup for lunch, the spoons we toss,
Mittens fight like they're a boss.
Chattering teeth, with every sip,
Frosty air, the life we grip.

When the sun peeks through the trees,
We cheer it on with frozen knees.
In this chill, we find our cheer,
Oh, winter days, you bring such sphere!

Still Waters Run Deep

A pond dressed white, it's quite a show,
Where ducks ski down, look at them go!
Snowflakes dance on water's crust,
Checkered mittens, gather dust.

Sliding, gliding, oops, I'll fall!
Winter's game, we skate and sprawl.
A friendly shove, with giggles bright,
Hilarity under crisp moonlight.

Icicles hang like teeth of fright,
But we don't let that stop our flight.
Building castles, proud and tall,
Then they crumble—oh, what a fall!

As the sun dips, hues adorn,
We share tales of winter's yarn.
With each glance, we laugh and leap,
In this chill, our hearts take a peek.

Adrift in Snowflakes

Frosty air, a fluffy mess,
Snowmen with carrot noses, no less.
With twinkling eyes, snowflakes tease,
Whispering secrets on the breeze.

Sleds go whizzing down the lane,
Woozy giggles, then we complain.
Frostbite toes, oh what a prank,
Yet we still love our cold, bright bank.

Upon the hill, we take our flight,
Flopping and flailing, oh what a sight!
Caught in laughter, the world feels right,
Winter wonderland, a snowy delight.

When shadows stretch and evening calls,
The night descends with sparkly spalls.
Together we dawdle, sip and share,
For in this cold, joy fills the air.

Hibernal Serenade

Snowflakes dance on sleepy roads,
Squirrels snooze in cozy abodes.
The cold wind whispers a frosty tease,
While penguins slide with stylish ease.

Puddles freeze like ice cream treats,
And snowmen sport their silly feats.
Icicles hang like toothy grins,
As winter's mischief surely begins.

Fires crackle with a gentle roar,
While hot cocoa spills on the floor.
Biting chills give rise to cheer,
And warm socks make us shed a tear.

Chairs piled high with laundry loads,
As we lounge in fuzzy codes.
In hats askew, we laugh and sway,
Winter's magic in a funny way.

A Symphony of Silence

The world wears white like a goofy clown,
Snow boots squeak; no one wears a frown.
Pines wear gowns of sparkling ice,
As rabbits hop and roll the dice.

Noses red, cheeks like cherries bright,
Snowball fights turn friends to fright.
Chattering teeth laugh in delight,
At all the chaos brought by night.

Winter's breath, a chilly blast,
But cocoa warms us; fun's unsurpassed.
Ear muffs hug our silly heads,
As we spin tales in cozy beds.

The quietude sings a frosty song,
While penguins waddle and don't feel wrong.
Ice slides beckon, do we dare?
Each slip and tumble, a laugh to share.

Bare Boughs in Twilight

Branches stretch with a frozen pose,
Where winter's creek merrily flows.
Cardinals laugh, red against the grey,
As they secretly plot their next play.

Footprints trace a silly dance,
In a snowstorm's bright expanse.
We chase each other, lose our hats,
Turn snowflakes into ponderous spats.

Evening draws with a twinkling gaze,
While snowflakes perform their fluttering phase.
Winter's giggles fill the night,
With chilly whims taking flight.

Under stars like twinkling eyes,
We huddle close while the cold wind cries.
In the hush, a chuckle's echo stays,
As winter crafts its funny displays.

Ethereal Winter Light

Frosty mornings, the world aglow,
A silent dance in the sun's soft show.
Laughter echoes off distant hills,
While snowmen dream of springs and frills.

Gloves wrong-handed make us sway,
As mittens lead us astray.
We chase the sun, yet it won't stay,
Leaving behind shadows of play.

Chill in the air adds bounce to our step,
Barely avoiding a frosty misrep.
Twinkling lights, like stars on ground,
As laughter in the crisp air surrounds.

Under lanterns, we share our plight,
In whimsical stories that feel just right.
Winter whispers sweet nothings near,
While funny moments bring us cheer.

Echoes of the Firewood

Crackling logs and popping sounds,
Squirrels dance like clowns around.
Chilly bunnies in coats so bright,
Poking fun at the cozy night.

The mistletoe hangs far too low,
Poor Uncle Fred keeps ducking slow.
With every sip, the laughter grows,
As snowflakes tickle his big red nose.

Fireside tales of growing gray,
Of pants that shrank from last buffet.
The woodpile smirks with every stack,
While grumpy chairs start talking back.

As blankets slip and pillows flop,
The giggles here just never stop.
In this chill, we're all quite bold,
Mismatched socks in colors sold.

The Art of Letting Go

Snowballs fly and laughter roars,
Snowman toppled, oh what a chore!
With carrot noses all a-bend,
Winter antics never end.

The scarf forgot its proper place,
Wrapped around a puppy's face.
He struts around, with pride that shows,
While grandma shakes her head and goes.

Hot cocoa spills, a flavored mess,
Trying to dance in all this stress.
Slippery socks on wooden floors,
Send us flying right outdoors.

But in this chill, we start to grin,
For each goof adds to our win.
Letting go, with laughter shared,
Brings warmth that winter never dared.

Frosted Memories

Pinecones dropping on my head,
Beards of frost in my warm bed.
Laughter echoes through the air,
As penguins slide without a care.

Mittens lost, where can they be?
I blame the cat—just watch and see.
A snowball thrown, my aim is poor,
I hit my dad, he shouts for more!

Pudding cups dance on the table,
Will they jump or will they fable?
In whipped cream fights, no one can win,
But giggles bring the fun back in.

Frozen noses count our glee,
In the chill, we'll always be.
Memories frost, then melt away,
Yet laughter stays, come what may.

Quiet Murmurs of Frost

Snowflakes whisper, soft and light,
   Jokes are told at noon's first light.
The cat makes snow angels, oh what fun!
   While children chase, we all just run.

With cookies baked and laughter loud,
   The dog jumps up and spins around.
He snags a treat, the cake's his prize,
   Covered in icing and sweet surprise.

Frosted mugs and feet on fire,
   Our cheering boosts the mood up higher.
Yet outside, the cold winds play,
   While inside warmth leads the way.

So gather 'round and hold on tight,
   Winter fun in the fading light.
With every giggle, let it flow,
   These cheerful moments softly glow.

Memories Encased in Ice

In winter's grip, I made a snowman,
He wore my hat; now he's the king of the land!
I offered him carrots, but he just stared,
Guess a snowman's diet is strictly unpaired.

Snowballs few; my aim was quite poor,
Hit the neighbor instead, now he has a sore.
With laughter echoing through the cold air,
I swear he threw one back, how unfair!

Sledding down slopes, I took quite a spill,
My backside froze; oh what a thrill!
Yet even the snowflakes giggle with glee,
When the ice is cracking, and so are my knees.

Hot cocoa waits, a promise so bold,
Marshmallows floating, a feast to behold.
I sip, and I laugh, for the season's a prank,
Life's too chilly to take it all blank.

Long Shadows on Frozen Paths

Upon the ice, my shadow stretches long,
Like a penguin slinking, I waddle along.
With twinkling laughter, I glide and I slip,
Making new friends with the frost on my lip.

The dog leaps and bounds, a furry delight,
Chasing the snowflakes, oh what a sight!
He tackles a mound – a mound of snow,
Now a white puppy, just ready to go!

My mittens are drenched, my cheeks rosy red,
As I stumble through snowbanks, over my head.
Each time I fall, I just giggle and grin,
Oh winter, you're wild — let the fun begin!

A hot tub awaits - running dinner bell,
With friends all around, it's warm as a spell.
But first, one last snowball, a playful attack,
I'll save you some hot cocoa - if you come back!

The Solitude of Distant Flakes

Snowflakes twirl and dance in the air,
They laugh silently, without any care.
Land on my nose, then vanish away,
Guess they have places to be — no delay!

Icicles hanging like teeth down below,
I fear they might drop, and give me a show.
But as I gaze longingly up at them,
I wonder if they too have a whimsical gem.

Each flake is unique, yet they all seem to freeze,
Chilling my laughter, my warmth, my ease.
"What's the hurry?" I ask all around,
While the world in white blankets keeps twirling down.

I'll build me a fort; it's a fortress of fun!
Laughing with snowmen, I'm never outdone.
With snowball fights and giggles galore,
In this frosty wonder, who could ask for more?

In the Embrace of White Silence

In winter's hush, my thoughts take to flight,
Footprints in snow lead me deep in delight.
Each crunch beneath, a symphony plays,
While squirrels ponder life — in a nutty daze.

Branches hang heavy, draped in soft white,
They whisper of secrets, wrapped up tight.
A twinkle of frost, as a chubby bird chirps,
Its songs bring a smile, while my nose does a burp!

I'm buried in snow; laughter's my prayer,
Snow angels flapping and losing all care.
With mittens as cushions, I flop and I roll,
Life's like a snowglobe, in the chilly console.

Giggles and grins float through the cold air —
Winter's embrace, a romantic affair.
With tea in my mug, all snuggled up tight,
I relish each chuckle; oh, what pure delight!

Items Lost in a Snowdrift

A mitten fell, it's not alone,
A sandwich lost, now overgrown.
A lost shoe sings a snowy tune,
Next to a happy, frozen raccoon.

A hat waves high in drifts so deep,
While socks conspire to take a leap.
A forgotten toy, buried snug,
With snowflakes piling, it gives a shrug.

Oh, when the thaw comes soft and slow,
What treasures found beneath the snow!
A scarf that danced with winter's breeze,
And socks that hide from cold with ease.

So if you lose a snack or thread,
Just laugh and know they're not quite dead.
For everything in snow shall play,
And make you smile on spring's first day.

Between the Silence

A flurry whirls with playful cheer,
While squirrels scold, their food too near.
The trees stand tall, in pajamas white,
As birds complain about their flight.

The air is crisp, sharp as a knife,
A snowman dreams of a snowwife.
The moon peeks through with a silly grin,
And giggles at the frosts within.

Clouds have gathered, forming snug,
Their fluffy bellies, a winter hug.
Meanwhile, snowflakes dance like fools,
Creating quite the scene of ghouls.

Between the peace, a laughter swells,
A snowball flies; we hear the yells!
So sip your cocoa, warm and nice,
And let the winter mischief entice.

Hallowed Ground of December

In December's grip, the ground is sweet,
With secrets hidden 'neath our feet.
The snowflakes swirl like tiny sprites,
Making this frosty world so bright.

A garden gnome, with a frown so bold,
Wonders where his nightcap went cold.
While snowmen argue over their hats,
And chase stray cats with acrobats.

In this hallowed place, giggles abound,
As children skate on frozen ground.
With cheeks like apples, they zip and zoom,
Creating frosty chaos, pure as bloom.

So let's raise a glass to the snowman's call,
To the laughter, the fun, the joy of all.
For every drift holds a silly mess,
And winter's charm is a lighthearted stress.

A Night of Glimmering Stars

A starry night with sparkles bright,
While snowflakes drift, a twinkling flight.
The moon, a jester, juggles light,
As rabbits hop in sheer delight.

Pine trees don their twinkling crowns,
In a gown of white, they dance around.
While polar bears play hide and seek,
Under the cosmic snowflake peak.

With whispers loud as winter's jest,
They tickle dreams with soft behest.
Where every flake holds a cheeky grin,
And laughter waltzes 'neath their skin.

So raise a toast to shimmering skies,
To chilly nights with fond surprise.
For in this frosty, glittering tease,
Winter brings joy, a heart at ease.

December's Cloak

Snowflakes tumble, soft like a cat,
Blanketing the world in a quiet spat.
I seek my glove, oh where can it be?
Winter's a thief, why's it messing with me?

Icicles dangle from rooftops tall,
Like nature's candy, waiting to fall.
Hot chocolate in hand, I take a big sip,
Oops! Now my nose is frosty and drip!

Sledding down hills, what a speed race,
Till I land face-first in a snow laced embrace.
Laughter erupts, it's all in good fun,
Till I roll over and melt in the sun!

The dog zooms by, a furry snowball,
Chasing after snowmen, he gives it his all.
I'm bundled up tight, a marshmallow puff,
But winter, dear friend, you're just never enough!

Shivering Dreams

A chill creeps in, like a sneaky mouse,
I'm wishing for warmth inside my house.
Pajamas layer like a cozy cake,
But even my hot tea starts to quake!

Dreams of summer flash like lightning bold,
While snowflakes dance, oh aren't they cold?
In slippers I shuffle, hear the wind howl,
This icy ballet sure makes me scowl!

Frosty windows sketch a frosty tell,
Of snowmen plotting in a wintry spell.
I swear I saw one start to do the twist,
But maybe that was just the cold's cruel mist!

As evening falls, I snuggle up tight,
With my cat who purrs, what a fuzzy sight.
We stare at the frost, my dear little friend,
Together we dream of warmth, the sweet end!

Whispers of a Frosty Night

The moon beams down on a snowy sea,
Where shadows of snowmen giggle with glee.
I peek outside, what's that? A prank?
A hidden snowball from the cheeky flank!

Beneath the stars, there's a comical sight,
Frosty critters join for a snowball fight.
Snowflakes twirl like they're at a ball,
Yet here I am, dodging them all!

With every crunch as I step outside,
I hear winter's whispers, they chide and slide.
Is that laughter I hear from the trees?
Or just the cold teasing, "Brrr, say cheese!"

My breath makes clouds in the chilly air,
While snowmen giggle without a care.
In this frozen world, I'm glad to play,
Even if my nose is turning away!

Pang of the Bitter Wind

Oh the winds howl like a howling dog,
Chasing my warm thoughts like a thick fog.
Scarf wrapped tight, I face the bite,
Slip on my boots, let's challenge the night!

The chill nips at my nose with sharp drills,
While snowflakes tickle my cheeks like frills.
I wave at neighbors stuck in a drift,
"Need a hot drink?" I inquire with a lift!

A plummet down stairs, oh what a sight,
Yikes! That was close, more laughter than fright.
Hot soup on the stove, a glorious steam,
Winter's a joke, or so it may seem!

I close my eyes, snug by the fire,
Dreaming of warmth, my heart's deep desire.
As winter cackles, I grin with delight,
For even in cold, I'll win this fight!

Amongst the Silent Pines

The trees wear white, quite the sight,
They dance with glee when the winds take flight.
Squirrels in mittens toss snowballs galore,
While the shy deer hide, peeking out for more.

A snowman grins with a carrot so bright,
But his button eyes freeze in the chilly night.
Frogs in their coats hop without a care,
Saying, "This icy breeze is simply quite rare!"

Chirping birds are on a vacation spree,
Sipping hot cocoa, not a worry, you'll see.
The sun plays hide and seek, what a fun game,
While everyone here shouts, "Winter, you're lame!"

Yet in this cold, laughter soon erupts,
As snowflakes fall, making all of us jump.
For amongst the pines, our spirits will soar,
In the land of frost, who can ask for more?

Numbed Together

Froze on my porch in last night's attire,
Mittens and boots, what a terrible wire!
I tripped on the ice, oh, what a delight,
Fell on my rear, now that's quite a sight!

Laughter erupts from my neighbor's loud den,
They joke, "Is it winter? Or simply just zen?"
We sip on our drinks, with noses all red,
This chilly affair makes us laugh instead!

The dog in the snow makes a snow angel's shape,
But now he's a ghost in a fluffy white cape.
"Bark twice if you're cold!" I tease with a smile,
He rolls in the snow; let's humor him a while!

Numbed toes and fingers, oh how we complain,
But inside we chuckle, it's all in the game.
I just spotted a penguin, or was that my friend?
Winter brings laughs that just never end!

Chilled Moments

In frosty pajamas, we bound down the lane,
Slipping and sliding, it's all just our gain.
The kids build a fort, using pillows and sheets,
While I warm up cocoa and snack on some treats.

Laughter erupts as we scatter some snow,
Snowballs in hand, watch that mischief grow!
But the dog pounds in, he's the creamiest pie,
And they all turn to freeze and say, "What a guy!"

With laughter and giggles, we share silly tales,
Like the time someone dressed up as cheerful snails.
We glance at the windows with frost on the glass,
And wonder how long till we see spring's green grass.

Yet for now, we bask in this chilled atmosphere,
Where laughter wraps 'round us like blankets, my dear.
Each moment, like snowflakes, shaping fun in the air,
In our winter wonderland, without a care!

Twilight's Frosted Breath

With each frosty breath, we jest and we play,
Waddle like penguins, who needs kids' ballet?
The twilight is crisp, with sparkles that twinkle,
As icicles hang like they're here for a sprinkle.

The neighbors have turned into snowmen today,
With carrots for noses and scarves made of hay.
Everyone's out for a chilly old chat,
While their noses are redder than my cooking fat!

Snowflakes fall softly, don't mind if they land,
On my hat, on my shoes, on my outstretched hand.
"Catch one!" I call, but they shimmer away,
Just like my old jokes that no one will say.

In this frosty twilight, we laugh till we cry,
As the moon casts a glow in the darkening sky.
There's magic in winter, a whimsical spree,
Our giggles the soundtrack, as free as can be!

Flights of Snowy Wishes

Tiny flakes dance, oh what a show,
Filling the air with a frosty glow.
Snowmen stand with a carrot nose,
As snowball fights hit a chilly pose.

Sleds zooming down, laughter rings clear,
Falling like snow, just trying to steer.
Frosty faces, cheeks all aglow,
Before you know it, it's time to go!

Hot cocoa waiting, marshmallows afloat,
Hot drinks are saviors in this frigid coat.
Chasing winter with mischievous glee,
Who knew cold days could be so carefree?

With shovels in hand, we dig out the fun,
Making our mark before spring has begun.
Oh winter, you sly little thief,
You've stolen our time, yet brought us relief!

Poised on the Edge of Day

Daylight whispers through the frost,
Cozy blankets in bed, at what cost?
Dreams of snow angels fly in our mind,
While snores of others make timing unkind.

The sun peeks out with a yawn and a stretch,
And all the hot coffee begins a sketch.
Cats in the window, searching for prey,
While dogs in their sweaters find new games to play.

With ice on the ground, take tiny steps slow,
Or you'll go sliding like a clumsy pro.
Laughter erupts from falls that ensue,
Funny how winter can leave us askew!

As the evening arrives, the moon starts to grin,
Casting shadows where mischief begins.
We toast to hot dinners beside the cold night,
What a delight, winter's quirky flight!

Moments Caught in Ice

Frozen moments, a snapshot of fun,
As kids on the rink dash, and then run.
With fanciful trips and graceful flips,
Joy ignites laughter, our chilly fingertips.

Sipping hot soup while we laugh 'bout our fate,
Stuck inside with a cat plotting to skate.
Frosty breath, with giggles in tow,
We'll remember these days and let the good times flow.

Snowflakes like feathers, soft in a flight,
Catching them twirling in the dimming light.
Glass windows freeze, drawings of dreams,
Life amidst winter is never quite what it seems.

But tales of the streaks we had on the ice,
Are funny by nature and oh-so-nice.
As seasons shall change, we will carry this cheer,
Moments that freeze; yet they warm all year!

Beneath the Silent Gaze of the Moon

A moonlit night with blankets that cling,
The sound of a snowball makes laughter ring.
Outside the window, a snowman winks,
And inside my mug, my cocoa still slinks.

Stars twinkle bright in their cotton candy,
With wishes for warmth and a day that's dandy.
The chill that bites isn't quite so mean,
When snowflakes laugh, the light can be seen.

Panic ensues when a dog does a dash,
Right through a pile that looks like a crash.
Cheeks all aglow, our spirits are high,
And plans for tomorrow leave us feeling spry.

So here's to the frosty, the funny and bright,
Underneath the moon's ever-watchful light.
We revel in moments caught mid-guffaw,
Winter, you charmer, you leave us in awe!

November's Painter's Touch

Squirrels wearing tiny hats,
Dashing through the snow so spry,
Painting trees with acorn splats,
As frosty winds laugh and sigh.

Pigeons in their fluffy coats,
Strutting like they own the park,
Waddling round in winter's boats,
While leaves now dance, devoid of lark.

Snowmen with their carrot noses,
Wink as kids all start to build,
Tickling toes and sniffly poses,
With cheeks as red as joy fulfilled.

Hot cocoa's rich, marshmallows float,
As laughter rings all through the chill,
Winter's bloom, a silly coat,
Brings warmth to hearts, a happy thrill.

Firelight's Flickering Peace

Crackling logs snort like a pig,
Dancing flames with shadows flirt,
Sweaters on that feel too big,
While cats puff up, they start to spurt.

Hot dogs roasting orange, bright,
S'mores melt into gooey bliss,
Whispers echo in the night,
As ghost stories take their twist.

Marshmallows tumble from the bag,
A sticky game of catch ensues,
Laughter blends with the sweet lag,
As frosty air inspires chews.

Blankets wrapped like big burritos,
Chasing shadows 'round the floor,
While we snuggle with our nachos,
Winter's charm demands encore.

Sighs of an Icebound World

Frosty windows, tiny breath,
Wrap us tight in chilly ties,
Snowflakes fall in flurries, death
To nerve-wracking, drifting sighs.

Penguins sliding belly-flop,
Jolly giggles fill the air,
Ice cream's what we want to swap,
Though it's freezing, we don't care!

Laughter bounces on the lake,
As snowballs fly and hit the tree,
Dense hats worn all in good sake,
While laughter reigns, we feel so free.

Winter's surprise, a playful tease,
With every step, crunching sound,
Giggles flung like tumbling leaves,
In icebound worlds, joy can be found.

Crystalline Solitude

Sparkling snowflakes tiptoe down,
Like shy dancers in a row,
Winter's gown, a frosty crown,
Tall trees wear their icy show.

Footprints lead to where? Who knows!
Yet laughter lingers in the chill,
As winter plays its quirky shows,
With every patch, a thrill to fill.

Mittens lost in the snowy maze,
As snowmen plot their great escape,
They giggle loud in frozen phrases,
Creating fun from chilly drape.

So let us slide and tumble down,
On icy paths with giggly trails,
In crystalline joy, we wear a frown,
And toast to winter's playful tales.

The Hush of Twilight's Chill

The snowflakes waltz, oh what a show,
As squirrels wear tiny scarves, don't you know?
The trees look shy, they shiver with grace,
While ice skates clamor, oh what a race!

Hot cocoa cheers while snowmen boast,
With carrot noses, they love to toast!
But watch your step, dear frosty friend,
Or you might slip and twist your blend!

Cats in mittens, oh what a sight,
Paws in the air, giving snowballs a fright!
While all around, the frosty morn,
The snowflakes giggle, and the world is reborn!

So dance with chill, let laughter ring,
In the frosty air, let your heart take wing.
For in this hush, with quirks and cheer,
Winter's a comedian, let's all draw near!

Frosted Silence in Each Breath.

Icicles dangle like nature's bling,
As penguins slide, they can't help but sing!
Footprints sparkle in the blanketed white,
Making snow angels, oh what a delight!

The winter sun beams with a frosty grin,
While hot soup bubbles, let the fun begin!
Giggling kids toss snow, unaware of the risk,
But who knew snowballs could be such brisk?!

With every breath, a cloud forms and fades,
Sending frosty whispers through icy glades.
A snowman frowns, has he lost his hat?
While his carrot nose is claimed by a cat!

So raise your mugs to this playful chill,
With laughter echoing over the hills!
Winter's a clown, with snow as his stage,
Together we'll dance, turning the page!

Whispers of Frost

The frostbit whispers tickle the air,
While frost-covered trees make a fuzzy lair.
A rabbit in sunglasses hops down the lane,
While laced with snow, he won't feel the pain!

The chill may bite, it's quite a prank,
Hot chocolate spills on the one who sank!
With sleigh bells ringing, oh what a noise,
As children giggle, playing with joys!

As ice sculptures gleam, they wave and dance,
Crafted with love, they take a chance.
Yet one cheeky snowman starts to sweat,
What a sight, but no one's upset!

With snowflakes twirling like ballerinas bright,
Winter's humor gives us pure delight.
So let's bundle up in this frosted delight,
And celebrate chuckles until day turns night!

Silence Beneath the Snow

In a blanket of white, the world takes a rest,
While squirrels prepare for their comedy fest.
The wind tells tales of a frosty affair,
As mittens and boots dance everywhere!

An old dog snorts while attempting to roll,
In fluffy white mounds, he takes on his goal.
Biding his time, he jumps into play,
But falls flat on his side, what a clumsy display!

The moon hangs low, casting snowflakes bright,
As deer twirl around in their frosty delight.
With each gentle howl, a joke fills the air,
As chilly breath whispers, "Don't you dare!"

So gather your friends 'neath this quiet glow,
Let's laugh at the frosty antics, oh so low.
For in this quiet where winter reigns,
The laughter of creatures is what still remains!

The Quietude of a Winter's Tale

Frosty whispers calm the air,
A snowman's hat is quite the flair.
Penguins in scarves wander to play,
While squirrels debate on who wins the day.

Chill pigeons gossip on the street,
While icicles form with their frosty feet.
A skating rink turns into a dance,
As kids spin 'round in a frozen trance.

Polar bears waltz in the bright,
Chasing snowballs with all of their might.
Snowflakes giggle as they pass by,
Daring hot cocoa to give it a try.

Mittens misplace themselves in the snow,
While scarves vie for the best status quo.
Frosted windows tell tales of cheer,
In a world that glimmers, so bright and sheer.

When Time Paused for Snowflakes

A flake floats down, striking a pose,
It tickles a cat and the fun just grows.
Time hangs still as cold winds sigh,
While dreams of sunbeams wave goodbye.

The sun wears glasses, too cool to shine,
While snowmen mock us in shapes so fine.
Kids throw snowballs with giggling glee,
As penguins plot their next cup of tea.

Frogs wearing boots, acting quite absurd,
Debate on flying but seldom heard.
A duck quacks loudly, "What's that you say?,"
While rabbits dance the cha-cha all day.

So here we stand, wrapped in warmth and cheer,
While winter's antics bring joy, bring fear.
At twilight time, the stars align,
A world of laughter, oh how divine!

Reflections on a Glassy Pond

A mirror of ice where ducks take their flight,
Waddling around in their coats, what a sight!
They quack about fashion, strutting their stuff,
In this frozen land, where it's cold and tough.

The fish hold their breath, they're quite in a thrall,
As cats on the bank debate fishing for all.
A beaver plays chess with the blue jays so bold,
While overhanging branches get kissed by the cold.

The breeze plays a tune with the trees as a choir,
Highlighting each note with its chilly desire.
While nearby a squirrel does backflips and twirls,
An acrobat legend among winter's pearls.

The pond says, "Hey, let's freeze this show!"
With dances of light and a snowfall glow.
So let laughter ring out, from the big to the small,
In this whimsical wonderland, there's joy for us all!

Solstice Reverie in the Glare of Cold

Snowflakes twinkle like lights on a tree,
Cackling at elves who sip cocoa with glee.
The stars make snowmen, all plump and round,
Whispering secrets, while giggles abound.

The moon wears a scarf and shivers with cheer,
Watching the rabbits serve hot soup from a pier.
Sledding down hills, with a splash and a dash,
Grinning like snowflakes, awaiting a crash.

Gnomes in red hats take part in the fun,
Juggling the snowballs, one by one.
As ice sculptures dance in the shimmering glow,
The world is in stitches, don't you know?

When winter exhibits its humorous flair,
Expect giggles and chuckles as we all share.
So raise a mug high, and let's toast the cold,
In laughter and warmth, let our stories unfold!

Milton Keynes UK
Ingram Content Group UK Ltd.
UKHW021939121124
451129UK00007B/150

9 789916 945827